SERJEANT FOR
THE COMMONS

House of Commons Library Documents
Published by HMSO (to 1997) and by The Stationery Office Limited (from 1997)

General Editors: David Menhennet (to 1990)
Chris Pond (from 1990)

Number	Title	
1	Acts of Parliament: some Distinctions in their Nature and Numbering	1955
2	A Bibliography of Parliamentary Debates of Great Britain	1967
3	The Mace in the House of Commons	1971
4	Official Dress worn in the House of Commons	1960
5	Access to Subordinate Legislation	1963
6	Ceremonial in the House of Commons	1967
7	The Journal of the House of Commons: A Bibliographical and Historical Guide	1971
8	Votes and Standing Orders of the House of Commons: The Beginning	1971
9	Erskine May's Private Journal 1857–1882: Diary of a Great Parliamentarian	1972
10	William Lambarde's Notes of the Procedures and Privileges of the House of Commons	1977
11	Ceremonial and the Mace in the House of Commons	1980
12	Erskine May's Private Journal 1883–1886	1984
13	Serjeant for the Commons	1986 *(3rd edition 1999)*
14	Secretaries to Mr Speaker	1986
15	English Constituency Histories 1265–1832	1986
16	Debates and Proceedings of the British Parliaments: A Guide to Printed Sources	1986
17	Observations, Rules and Orders of the House of Commons: An Early Procedural Collection	1989
18	The Royal Mace in the House of Commons	1990
19	Chaplains to Mr Speaker: Religious Life of the House of Commons	1991
20	In Parliament 1939–1950	1991
21	The House of Commons Library: A History	1991
22	Secretary to the Speaker: Ralph Verney's Papers	1999

HOUSE OF COMMONS
LIBRARY DOCUMENT No. 13

(Third Edition)

General Editor: Chris Pond

Serjeant for the Commons

Peter Thorne
formerly Serjeant at Arms

revised by

Michael Cummins
Deputy Serjeant at Arms

London: The Stationery Office

Applications for reproduction should be made to the General Editor at
The House of Commons Library

First Edition 1985
Third Edition 1999

ISBN 0 10 850651 7

Published by The Stationery Office Limited
and available from:

The Publications Centre
(Mail, telephone and fax orders only)
PO Box 276, London SW8 5DT
General Enquiries *Lo-call* 0345 58 54 63
Order through the Parliamentary Hotline *Lo-call* 0345 02 34 74
Fax orders 0171 873 8200

The Stationery Office Bookshops
123 Kingsway, London WC2B 6PQ
0171 242 6393 Fax 0171 242 6394
68-69 Bull Street, Birmingham B4 6AD
0121 236 9696 Fax 0121 236 9699
33 Wine Street, Bristol BS1 2BQ
0117 926 4306 Fax 01179 294515
9-21 Princess Street, Manchester M60 8AS
0161 834 7201 Fax 0161 833 0634
16 Arthur Street, Belfast BT1 4GD
0123 223 8451 Fax 0123 223 5401
The Stationery Office Oriel Bookshop
The Friary, Cardiff CF1 4AA
0122 239 5548 Fax 01222 384347
71 Lothian Road, Edinburgh EH3 9AZ
0131 228 4181 Fax 0131 622 7071

The Parliamentary Bookshop
12 Bridge Street, Parliament Square,
London SW1A 2JX
Telephone orders 0171 219 3890
General enquiries 0171 219 3890
Fax orders 0171 219 3866

Accredited Agents
(see Yellow Pages)

and through good booksellers

Contents

Illustrations

Foreword
to the First Edition

IN THIS PUBLICATION SIR PETER THORNE, SERJEANT AT Arms, House of Commons from 1976 to 1982, gives an historical review of the Serjeant at Arms and his Department from the appointment of Nicholas Maudit in 1415 to the present day. In Chapter 6, he touches on some aspects of the Department's work in modern times.

The Library and Serjeant at Arms' Departments greatly appreciate this further contribution from Sir Peter, who has drawn on his many years' experience of the Parliamentary scene with his usual skill.

We are grateful to Dr Chris Pond for seeing this publication through the press.

December 1985

Victor Le Fanu
Serjeant at Arms
David Menhennet
Librarian

Foreword to the Third Edition

In the fourteen years that have passed since the first edition, many changes to practices and personnel have taken place. The ancient office of Serjeant at Arms of the Commons has changed too, and has in particular assumed the responsibility, through the Parliamentary Works Directorate, maintaining and planning extensions to Members' accommodation in the Palace itself and in the outbuildings. This revision has been undertaken by Michael Cummins, the present Deputy Serjeant, to whom our thanks are due.

CCP 1999

Updated Extract from House of Commons Manual of Procedure in the Public Business

Chapter 4—Officers and Departments of the House

29.   The Serjeant at Arms is appointed by the Crown under a warrant from the Lord Chamberlain, and by letters patent under the great Seal which direct him 'to attend upon Her Majesty's person when there is no Parliament; and at the time of every Parliament, to attend upon the Speaker of the House of Commons'; but after his appointment he is the servant of the House, and may be removed for misconduct. The mace—originally the emblem of office of a Royal Serjeant at Arms—has become the symbol of the powers and privileges of the House.

The police and security staff on duty in the House of Commons are under the direction of the Serjeant at Arms. He regulates, under the Speaker, the admission of persons to the Press Gallery and Lobby, and has control of the arrangements for the admission of strangers.

The Serjeant at Arms is also housekeeper of the House of Commons. He is assisted by a Deputy Serjeant, and three Assistant Serjeants. He sees to the maintenance of order in the lobbies and passages of, and approaches to, the House, and may be regarded as representing the executive authority of the House.

In view of his responsibilities in connection with the administration of the House, the Serjeant at Arms is in attendance at meetings of the Select Cormmittees on Administration, Accommodation and Works, Information, and on Finance and Services.

Introduction

To THE CASUAL OBSERVER OF THE PARLIAMENTARY scene, the three senior officers of the Commons—the Speaker, the Clerk and the Serjeant at Arms—share two disadvantages: they are required to wear an antique form of court dress, and their titles are extremely misleading. But, whereas the Speaker does act, when necessary, as the spokesman of the House, and the Clerk's duties include an element of clerical work, there is little—except his sword—to connect the Serjeant with the mounted bodyguard of the early Plantagenet kings, in which role the Serjeants at Arms first became prominent.

While the Serjeant's present day duties are shown in outline in the preceding extract, the following chapters describe the role of the early Serjeants in the Commons: their varying methods of appointment and the differences in the terms of their patents; how the Commons based their penal jurisdiction on the power of arrest of a royal Serjeant at Arms and how the Mace was transformed from the Serjeant's emblem of office into the symbol of the powers and privileges of the House; how the Commons have employed the Serjeant in asserting these privileges; and how the Serjeant's other role as Housekeeper has developed in a House chronically short of accommodation.

This booklet only deals in passing with present day ceremonial. This is described more fully in *Ceremonial and the Mace in the House of Commons* published as House of Commons Library Document No. 11. Further information on, and history of, the Mace can be found in *The Royal Mace*, House of Commons Library Document No. 18.

Chapter One

Beginnings

EDWARD I FORMED A BODYGUARD OF TWENTY Serjeants at Arms in 1279[1]; previously they only seem to have been used as the permanent element in the garrisons of royal castles, or as an escort for traitors or other prisoners being brought to London. He was in no way an innovator, as King Philip Augustus of France had created his bodyguard of Serjeants at Arms some eighty years previously in the Holy Land as a protection against attacks by the Assassins of Alamut[2]. The only bodyguard that Richard Coeur de Lion, King Philip's fellow Crusader, is known to have possessed was composed of renegade Saracens[3].

The English bodyguard's strength was later increased to 30[4], and by 1415, when one of their number was appointed to attend upon all the Parliaments 'as Serjeant at Arms for the Commons coming thereto'[5], new responsibilities had been thrust upon these 'armed servants', so that they were no longer confined to the straightforward bodyguard duties of the Sovereign's mounted escort, but had become figures of considerable controversy in the administrative structure of the country.

These royal Serjeants' immediate availability as a strong-arm party had led to their being assigned a variety of tasks, which Professor Tout in his work on Mediaeval Administrative History described as 'the ubiquitous activities of the King's Serjeant at Arms who collected loans and taxes, impressed men and ships, served on local commissions and in all sorts of ways interfered with the course of local administration and justice.'[6].

They had also incurred the wrath of the Commons: on four occasions between 1386 and 1397 the Rolls of Parliament show that there were protests to Richard II about the arbitrary behaviour of his Serjeants at Arms, about their crimes of extortion and oppression, and about the King's failure to control them[7]. Thereafter the complaints cease, perhaps because the incoming House of Lancaster had the Serjeants under tighter control, perhaps because the Commons were beginning to negotiate for a Serjeant of their own. In 1415, the year of Agincourt, they successfully petitioned for the appointment of Nicholas Maudit, one of the existing royal Serjeants. It would be pleasant to be able to confirm that the early Serjeants led useful and busy lives in the service of the Commons: presumably they did so, or the Commons would not have gone to the trouble of insisting that they had a Serjeant. But although we know something about their method of appointment, there is virtually nothing on the record about the actual use the Commons made of their Serjeants for the first hundred years or so.

They were chosen to 'attend' or 'be attendent upon' the Commons or the Speaker, but there is no indication as to how they were employed in that capacity until the Ferrers case of 1545, when the use of a royal Serjeant's power of arrest without a warrant became a fundamental step in the development of the penal jurisdication of the Commons.

Serjeants at Arms had in fact been used in the running of some of the earliest Parliaments long before the Knights and Burgesses (i.e. the House of Commons) formed a permanent element in those assemblies. In the *Modus Tenendi Parliamentum*[8], written some time between 1294 and 1327, there are references to Serjeants at Arms having been posted to keep order in the approaches to the Parliament and to admit those who had business there. But it would appear from the use of the past tense by the writer of the *Modus* that the King's Serjeants had been largely replaced by ushers (*hostiarrii*), and that this innovation did not find favour 'because by right, the door of Parliament ought not to be shut, but guarded by ushers and King's Serjeants at Arms'[9]. We can only guess at the reasons for this change: one may have been the difference in cost of employing an usher instead of a Serjeant, as the annual livery of the latter was more than three times as expensive as that of an usher.

At approximately the same time there is a mention of a Royal Serjeant at Arms being appointed by the King to 'l'office de porter la masse en notre dite cité'[10] of London. Although this entry does not indicate what the office of carrying the Mace entailed (it was apparently not the first appointment of this kind to be made), its wording suggests that there was already a ceremonial factor in the attachment of a Serjeant to an outside body like the City. There is however no mention of any ceremonial with the Mace in the Commons until the first year of Queen Elizabeth I's reign The first time the Mace appears in any account of ceremonial in the House of Commons is in D'Ewes' reference to Gargrave, who on being approved by the Queen as Speaker in 1558: '. . . . . departed with the other Members of the House of Commons to their own House, the Serjeant of the same carrying the Mace all the way before the said Speaker'.[11]

In addition to duties allotted by the Commons, these early Serjeants were still expected to carry out the various tasks described by Professor Tout earlier in this chapter. Nicholas Maudit's appointment to attend upon the Commons did not preclude him from being used by the King on certain tasks which had very little to do with the Commons. One such duty—in connection with King Henry V's campaign in France—was 'to seize all ships and other vessels of the realm and foreign ports of the portage of 20 tons and above now in the River Thames and from there . . . to the port of Newcastle . . . and to take those of the realm to the port of Southampton'.[12] In the following year he was 'to arrest John Bailly of Battersea, co. Surrey, and bring him immediately before the King in Chancery'[13].

By the beginning of the fifteenth century the Commons had already acquired a Speaker and a Clerk; and their decision to petition for the appointment of a Serjeant may well have arisen from the need they felt for an official to look after the non-procedural aspects of their existence. Mediaeval institutions such as abbeys, whose *raison d'etre* was not a warlike one, appointed a lay official called an 'advocatus' who was responsible for their protection and the administration of their lands[14]. In choosing Nicholas Maudit, the Commons may have decided that he possessed the qualities needed to carry out those functions of an *advocatus*—their defender and their agent in secular affairs—which were relevant to their developing needs.

NOTES TO CHAPTER ONE

[1]Household ordinance of 1279 quoted in T. F. Tout: *Chapters in the Administrative History of Mediaeval England*: Manchester 1928–37 Vol. II. p. 163. There are frequent references in Vols. III to V of the *Calendar of Liberate Rolls* to the payment of Serjeants at Arms in garrison at Windsor and the Tower of London

[2]Père Daniel: *Histoire de la Milice Française.* Paris 1721. Tome 2. p. 92.

[3]Sir Maurice Powicke: *Scottish Historical Review.* Vol. 8. 1991.

[4]T F. Tout. *The Place of the Reign of Edward II in English History.* Manchester 1936. p. 253.

[5]*Calendar of Close Rolls:* Henry V 1413–1419 p. 207

[6]Tout *op. cit.* (1928–37) Vol. IV p. 44.

[7]*Rotluli Parliamentarum* Vol. III. 1386 p. 223; 1389 p. 265; 1393 p. 318; 1397 p. 354.

[8]*Modus Tenendi Parliamentum.* Record Commission Edition ed. T. D. Hardy. London 1846 pp. 36,38.

[9]*Ibid* p. 38.

[10]Corporation of London Record Office: *Letter Book* F. f206.

[11]Sir Simonds D'Ewes: *Journal of all the Parliaments during the Reign of Queen Elizabeth.* London 1682 p. 43.

[12]*Calendar of Patent Rolls:* Henry V. 1413–1416 pp. 342–343.

[13]*Ibid* p. 413. Maudit may have had a personal interest in this case, as he owned lands in Battersea.

[14]S. M. Wood. *English Monasteries and their Patron.* Oxford 1955. p. 2.

Chapter Two

Methods of Appointment

WHEN DISRAELI TOLD THE HOUSE IN 1875 THAT THE appointment of the Serjeant 'is the gift and entirely in the gift of Her Majesty'[1], he was echoing a statement made by John Pym in the reign of Charles I. There had been a discussion about the method of appointing the Clerk and the Serjeant: Pym had explained that whereas the Clerk was chosen by the Commons, the 'Serjeant is an ensign of honour with which the King has been pleased to grace the Parliament'[2].

The practice of the Sovereign choosing the Serjeant for the Commons does not, however, quite go 'back to the early History of Parliament' as stated by the Prime Minister in 1962[3], but to a decision by Henry VIII. Before that it seems to have been the custom for the Commons to petition the Sovereign to appoint a Serjeant of their own choosing.

The Calendar of Close Rolls for the reign of Henry V shows that in April 1415 'at the special petition of the Commons . . . the King granted that the said Nicholas Maudit should during his life attend upon all his Parliaments . . . as Serjeant at Arms for the Commons coming thereto'[4] which is much the same as the wording in the Calendar of Patent Rolls of the previous year 'Grant at the supplication of the Commonalty of the realm in the present Parliament that the Kings Esquire, Nicholas Maudit, one of the King's Serjeants at Arms, shall be intendent at all Parliaments for the Commonalty coming to the Parliaments . . .'[5]

Nicholas Maudit died some time before 1440. For the next 20 years or so there is no record of another Serjeant being appointed to be 'intendent' on the Commons, although their tasks may have been performed by ushers or 'valets' of the Parliament Chamber.

In 1467, there is a reference in the Rolls of Parliament to the appointment of another Serjeant 'John Bury, one of the King's Sergeauntes at Armes, chosen by the Commons of England to entend to the same Commons in tyme of every Parliament'[6], and this wording is used in reference to Bury's immediate successors. This formula of being 'chosen by the Commons of England' figures for the last time in a warrant to John Harper[7] who served the Commons for much of Henry VII's reign.

There is nothing to show why the change was made, but the patent of the next Serjeant—John Smythe—who was appointed two years after Henry VIII succeeded, merely states that he was to be 'the Serjeant at Arms attending

2. Two contemporary illustrations of Serjeants at Arms in the reigns of Henry VII and Henry VIII

the King when there is no Parliament, and the Speaker of the Commons when there is'[8]. Smythe's patent omits all reference to his being chosen by the Commons, and one can only speculate on the reasons that led Henry to take the power of selection away from the Commons.

The instruction that the Serjeant was to attend upon the Speaker first appears in a grant to Maurice Gethyn, who followed John Bury in 1471, 'he shall be attendant on the Speaker of Parliament as John Bury lately was'[9]. This specific assignment to the Speaker, which is not made in the case of the Clerk of the House, has been repeated in the grants or patents of all succeeding Serjeants down to the present time.

This duty to attend upon the Speaker does not appear to have made much difference to the Serjeant's responsibilities towards the Commons as a whole. While John Harper is described in one entry in the Rolls of Parliament as 'one of our Serjeauntes at Armes, specially attending upon the Speaker of oure Parliament'[10], a few pages earlier he is referred to as one of the King's Serjeants at Arms 'chosen by the said Commons to entend the same Commons in the tyme of every Parliament'[11].

This twofold responsibility to the Speaker and the House continues to this day: the letters patent appointing a new Serjeant specify that he is to attend upon the Speaker, but elsewhere—as in the Standing Orders of the House—he is described as 'the Serjeant at Arms attending the House of Commons'[12] and is expected to carry out the directions of both the Speaker and the House.

In 1962, the Prime Minister[13] told the House that the Sovereign was willing to enter into consultation with the Speaker to ensure that future Serjeants would have the approval of the House; and the Commons' former right to choose their Serjeants was restored.

NOTES TO CHAPTER TWO

[1] Quoted in HC Vol. 666.

[2] *Journal of Sir Simonds D'Ewes.* Ed. W. Notestein, Yale 1923. p. 264, note 12.

[3] *HC Deb* 8 November 1962, Vol. 666 Col. 1155.

[4] *Calendar of Close Rolls* Henry V 1413–1419 p. 207.

[5] *Calendar of Close Rolls* Henry V 1413–1416 p. 196.

[6] *Rotuli Parliamentorum* Vol. V p. 574 Col. b.

[7] *Rotuli Parliamentorum* Vol. V p. 339 Col. a.

[8] *Letters and Patents of the Reign of Henry VIII* 1517–1518 Vol. 2. Part 2. p. 1094.

[9] *Calendar of Patent Rolls* Edward IV and Henry VII 1467–1477 p. 265.

[10] *Rotuli Parliamentorum* Vol. VI p. 344 a.

[11] *Rotuli Parliamentorum* Vol. VI p. 339 (a).

[12] *Standing Orders of the House of Commons.* Passim.

[13] *HC Deb* 11 December 1962. Vol. 669, cols. 209–210.

Chapter Three

The Mace and its Uses

FOR NEARLY A CENTURY BEFORE THE COMMONS acquired the services of Nicholas Maudit, the Mace had become the recognised emblem of a royal Serjeant at Arms, and an object to be regarded with awe. As proof that the Serjeants were acting as the King's agents, the royal arms were stamped on their Maces, so that, in an age when few men could read or write, they effected their arrests by showing their Maces, and not by producing any form of written warrant.

In the early fifteenth century, Serjeants' Maces were not the cumbersome things they later became, and Nicholas Maudit's Mace, which is portrayed on his memorial brass in Wandsworth Parish Church, is little bigger than a modern police truncheon.

The Serjeants' Maces had originally been part of the normal equipment of mounted men at arms, together with their lances and swords and armour. The Mace is, of course, only a development of the club, which is the oldest of weapons; but whereas wooden clubs became obsolescent when metal cutting and thrusting weapons made their appearance, the iron battle Mace with its flanged or spiked head was in turn introduced as an effective counter measure against the mail or plate armour that would turn a sword cut or spear thrust. Maces were predominantly a close combat weapon of the mounted knight or man at arms, and because they were short and handy they were especially suitable for those who had to command as well as fight.

There is some evidence that ornamental maces were first encountered during the Crusades amongst the Saracens, whose leaders are portrayed as carrying ceremonial Maces; and it is not improbable that, from their use by a highly civilised enemy, they acquired a certain prestige in addition to their purely functional value. In the later Middle Ages, their use as emblems of office, not only of the royal Serjeants-at-Arms but of city and borough officials as well, spread rapidly throughout England; and in this way maces joined those other club-like insignia—sceptres and rods, staffs and verges, crosiers, wands and batons—that have been used since the dawn of history to denote spiritual or temporal authority.

Whatever the practice may have been at the beginning of the 15th century, there seem to have been fewer and fewer arrests of 'traitors' carried out by the Serjeants at Arms during the next hundred years. To an increasing extent the responsibility for making arrests of this kind was transferred to the

3. A seventeenth century print in the House of Commons of the Serjeant at the Bar of the House with a prisoner

Gentlemen of the Privy Chamber, and, as indicated in Chapter I, the Commons do not appear to have used their Serjeant's power of arrest without a warrant until the Ferrers case of 1545.

This occurred when a member, Ferrers, was arrested for debt by the City authorities, and the Commons ordered their Serjeant, St. John, to secure his release. When St. John reached the City, he was assaulted by the Counter Clerks—the City officials—and had to defend himself with the Mace, which was damaged in the brawl. The Sheriffs refused to help him, and St. John returned to the Commons, where he made his complaint. The Commons ordered him to go back and fetch not only Ferrers, but all the other offenders as well, and to summon the Sheriffs and the Counter Clerks to appear before the Speaker the next morning. They did so and were committed to the Tower. Hollinshead's account says that 'They of the Commons House . . . being of the clear opinion that all commandments proceeding from the Neather House were to be done and executed by their Serjeant without writ, only by show of his Mace which was his warrant'.[1]

The Ferrers incident was notable because it was the first case that Elizabethan antiquaries could quote of the Commons controlling and managing its privilege of freedom from arrest and molestation. They could not have done so without the open support of the King; and it is conceivable

that Henry VIII personally encouraged the Commons not only to vindicate their privilege without going to the Courts of Law, but also to adopt an already obsolescent process in asserting their rights. This was to make use of a royal Serjeant at Arms to punish offenders, on the strength of the authority that was originally delegated to him by the Crown and symbolised by the Royal Arms on his Mace.

The next stage in the relationship between the Serjeant and the penal jurisdiction of the Commons was the introduction of the Speaker's Warrant to the Serjeant at Arms for taking offenders into custody.

The Select Committee inquiring in 1845 into the Howard v. Gossett case could not find any examples of such warrants before the reign of James I, and reported that 'The Practice of the House, in earlier times appears to have been to arrest without a written warrant. In these cases the Serjeant with the Mace was the sole indication of its will'[2]

The Speaker's Warrant seems therefore to have originated in a paradoxical situation that developed during the early seventeenth century Ever-increasing importance was then being attached to the Mace as the corporate symbol of the power and authority of the House, and this had led experts over a number of years to argue that the Commons could not be properly constituted if the Mace were not present. In the Commons Journal of 16 May 1614, there is, for instance, a reference to the Serjeant at Arms being sent to bring some 'King's learned Counsel' to the House: 'The Serjeant sent with his Mace for them; and questioned, whether any may speak whilst the Mace is gone and overruled, they may'.[3]

During the next generation the theorists still seem to have been in some doubts as to whether the Mace was absolutely necessary for the conduct of business, for in 1640 Sir Thomas Peyton reported that 'Mr. Pym said . . . it is a new doctrine, that wee can doe nothing without a Speaker, or the Mace';[4] but by the end of the century it seems to have been generally accepted that the Mace must be brought into the House before the Commons could consider themselves properly constituted. This new concept, however, came into conflict with the practice whereby the Serjeant was sent off with his Mace whenever the Commons required the attendance of a person at the Bar.

Some solution had then to be found if the proceedings of the House were not to be interrupted each time that the Serjeant was ordered to bring someone to the Bar. The device of the Speaker's Warrant to the Serjeant at Arms was therefore adopted, and this document not only ordered the Serjeant to take persons into custody but also required the civil authorities to offer him all the assistance he needed in carrying out this task. Thus the Mace could remain in the Chamber while the Serjeant at Arms was enabled to perform his mission armed with all the powers he would have possessed had he taken a Royal Mace with him.

Although the Commons, through the introduction of the Speaker's Warrant, took over many of the powers that had previously been notionally vested in the person of a royal Serjeant-at-Arms, the direct relationship

5. Cartoon, by 'H.B.', of the Speaker's procession, c. 1830 with Henry Seymour and Speaker Manners-Sutton *(from a print in the HC Library)*

Make way for
THE SPEAKER.

between the Serjeant and the penal jurisdiction of the House has not been completely ended.

The Serjeant—who is appointed by the Sovereign to attend upon the Speakers 'at the time of every Parliament' but 'to attend upon Her Majesty's person when there is no Parliament'—[5] still returns the Mace to the Jewel House when Parliament is prorogued or dissolved, and himself reverts, in theory, to the Royal Household as a Serjeant at Arms in Ordinary. Offenders committed by the Commons are automatically discharged from their place of imprisonment on prorogation, and the ability of the Commons to punish by imprisonment lapses when the Serjeant at Arms and the Mace are absent. The House of Commons' power to commit is co-terminous with the Serjeant's formal attendance on the House.

For more details about the Mace, the reader is referred to *The Royal Mace in the House of Commons* by P. F. Thorne (HC Library Document No. 18, 1989).

NOTES TO CHAPTER THREE

[1]John Hatsell: *Precedents*. London 1818 Vol. I p. 54.
[2]*Select Committee on Printed Papers. 2nd Report* (Parl. Papers, 1845, (HC 397) xiii. 233).
[3]*Commons Journals*. I. 486 (16 March 1614).
[4]*Journal of Sir Simonds D'Ewes*. Ed. W. Notestein, Yale 1923, p. 264 in note.
[5]*Serjeant at Arms Warrant*.
[6]Edward Colman, Serjeant at Arms 1775–1805 *(from a painting by Karl Anton Hickel in the Serjeant's Office)*.

Chapter Four

Orders of the House

I N 1884, IN WHAT WAS TO BE ONE OF THE LAST GREAT privilege cases fought in the Courts, Bradlaugh brought an action to enable him to sit and vote in the House as Member for Northampton, without having to take the statutory oath on the Bible. The defendant in the case was the Serjeant at Arms, Sir Ralph Gossett, and Lord Chief Justice Coleridge explained the reason for this: 'the Houses of Parliament cannot act by themselves as a body: they must act by officers; and the Serjeant at Arms is the legal and recognised officer of the House of Commons to execute its orders. I entertain no doubt that the House has a right to decide on the subject matter, have decided it, and have ordered their officer to give effect to their decision. He is protected by their decision.'[1]

In the eyes of the Judges of the Queen's Bench, it was a matter for the House to decide, and for the Serjeant, their executive officer, to take the necessary action: from the point of view of the Serjeant at Arms, however, the situation is not always as simple as that, and there have been times when the Commons have seemed less than perfect employers. This chapter shows that, on occasion, it has been dangerous as well as difficult to carry out the orders of the House; and that the Serjeant is unable to query these orders however ill-judged they may be. This principle of 'Theirs not to reason why' has become the normal practice ever since the Commons sought to imprison a Serjeant who had tried to use his discretion when faced with orders of doubtful legality and which would nowadays be considered unconstitutional. On the other hand, the Commons have failed to protect a Serjeant who had exceeded his duties and who was found to have acted *ultra vires*.

The Burdett case of 1810 was a classic example of the Serjeant and the House getting themselves into a dangerously embarrassing position. Sir Francis Burdett, Member for Westminster and the idol of the London mob, had made himself so unpopular with the Government that they decided to have him punished by the House for a breach of privilege. Initially, he eluded arrest by moving between his houses in Piccadilly and Wimbledon; and Francis Colman, the Serjeant, incurred the displeasure of the Speaker by not breaking in and serving the warrant. The legal position was obscure, and neither the Speaker nor the Attorney General were prepared to guarantee that the Serjeant would have immunity for his actions. Burdett then established himself in his home in Piccadilly, and the Government steeled

itself to use whatever force was necessary. Speaker Abbott accordingly instructed the Serjeant to effect an entrance into Burdett's home, and convey him to the Tower.

In view of the temper of the mob, the military was summoned in aid of the civil power, and eventually Burdett was handed over to the Governor of the Tower. But it had taken two battalions of Foot Guards and two regiments of Cavalry to escort the Serjeant's coach with Burdett through the crowd: the Life Guards had twice to charge down Piccadilly, and a number of people had been killed.

Again in 1851 the Serjeant was in difficulties when the House issued an ill-conceived order, in connection with the St. Albans case. Two absconders took refuge in Boulogne, and the Assistant Serjeant was sent on a fruitless mission to bring them back in custody, although it should have been clear to the House that the French police would not co-operate in a case of this kind.

The fate of Sir James Northfolk in 1675 is an awful warning to all Serjeants at Arms who might feel like querying their orders. During the course of a quarrel between Lords and Commons, Northfolk had been instructed to arrest four counsel who were appearing in a case in the House of Lords. He had second thoughts about the propriety of holding them in custody, and decided to release them: this infuriated the Commons who ordered him to be committed to the Tower, and asked Charles II to appoint another Serjeant.[2]

Nor do the Commons necessarily protect a Serjeant who has acted *ultra vires*. Serjeant Topham, who had made something of a name for himself by the zeal with which he carried out arrests, was fined £500—a very large sum in those days—for holding an Under Sheriff in custody after the House had been prorogued, and therefore after Topham's power of arrest, on behalf of the Commons, had lapsed.[3] It is perhaps ironic that the arrest of Milton in 1660—the most famous of all persons to have been taken into custody—does not seem to have provoked any criticism except that the fees which the Serjeant charged on Milton's release were considered somewhat excessive.[4]

In recent years the Serjeant's tasks outside the House have been mainly involved in ensuring the attendance of persons at the Bar of the House, or as witnesses in front of Select Committees or in the production of papers for them; normally this is done by his Clerk in Charge who is the Warrant Officer of the House serving on those concerned the appropriate orders.

Inside the Chamber, however, the Serjeant's actions either in pursuance of Standing Orders, or on the direction of the Speaker, attract the notice of the media from time to time. One Standing Order[5] instructs him to take into custody anybody who misconducts themselves in the Gallery, which

7. Francis Colman and Sir Francis Burdett

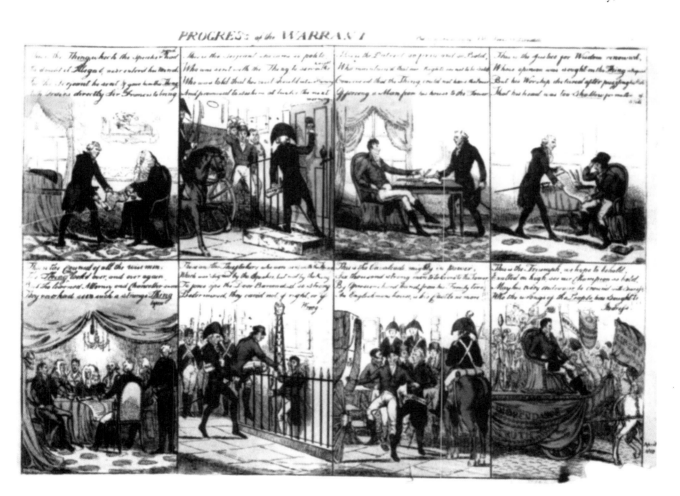

8. 'Vanity Fair' cartoon of Lord Charles Russell—1873 (print in the S at A's collection entitled "This Fell Serjeant—strict in his arrest")

occurs when a stranger decides to create a demonstration or other form of disorder and has to be removed and held in custody by the Police until the rising of the House.

Mercifully, the Standing Order authorising the Serjeant to use force—if the Speaker so directs—against a Member who refuses to withdraw from the Chamber[6] has not been used since 1931: in the last 50 years Members have always left the Chamber when 'named' by the Speaker, and when summoned by the Serjeant to withdraw. This Standing Order was instituted only in the last century, and its continued existence is something of a reproach, as a Speaker would not need the powers in a House whose Members could discipline themselves.

Order-keeping in the chamber frequently throws up new problems[7]. In 1980 an incident occurred when a group of Members prevented Black Rod getting beyond the Bar of the House to deliver his message until the Government had acceded to their requests; and on another occasion the Serjeant had to summon three Members to withdraw: not only were they the first Members to have been 'named' when seated upstairs in the Members' side gallery, but they comprised the entire strength of one parliamentary party.

On the other hand, a procedure which appears dormant can be brought into play again. Henry VIII gave an example when he encouraged the Commons to send their Serjeant to effect the arrests in the Ferrers Case,

9. Sir David Erskine, from a sketch in the Daily Graphic (1902).

10. Mr. John Junor being heard by the House on 24 January 1957 (Cartoon from Punch) Note that artistic licence has placed Mr Junor in front of the Mace instead of at the Bar of the House, some way further back.

"When did you last see your proprietor?"

11. The defeat of obstruction in the House of Commons—removal of Mr Parnell by Order of the Speaker by Sir Ralph Gossett, Serjeant at Arms, 1881.

thereby surprising the City authorities by the sudden reactivation of an archaic practice. In the early 1980s the Speaker employed a similarly ancient tactic in securing the withdrawal of a Member without 'naming' him. He did this by ordering the Serjeant to 'ensure' that the Honourable Member complied with the Speaker's direction to withdraw—a method that had not been used for over 80 years.

NOTES TO CHAPTER FOUR

[1]Queen's Bench (1884) Vol. XII p. 276.

[2]*Commons Journals* 27 Car. II 1675 pp. 350, 351.

[3]*Commons Journals* 10th July 1689 and Luttrell's Relations Vol 1. p. 211, 1682.

[4]*Commons Journals* 15 December 1660. David Masson: *Life of John Milton*, London 1880 Vol. VI. p.195.

[5]*Standing Orders of the House of Commons* (1989) (S.O. No. 141).

[6]*Ibid* (S.O No. 43(4)).

[7]See also *Disciplinary and Penal Powers of the House of Commons* (House of Commons Public Information Office Factsheet No. 63, 1993).

Chapter Five

The Serjeant and the House's Premises

THE 1800 ACT FOR ESTABLISHING CERTAIN REGULA-TIONS in the Offices of the House of Commons was the first major attempt to reorganise the administration of the House of Commons. It set up a body of Commissioners to supervise the remuneration of the senior Officers of the House, and to change it from a fee to a salary earning basis. Another Act, of 1812, defined more closely the duties and authority of the principal officers, including a prohibition on future Clerks exercising their office by Deputy, and on the Serjeant appointing somebody other than himself to act as Housekeeper[1].

Although the Act of 1812 said that the offices of Serjeant at Arms and Housekeeper of the House of Commons 'now and for a long time past have been holden conjointly by the same person' there are no precise references to the Serjeant's duties as Housekeeper before 1549, when St. John—the Serjeant in the Ferrers case—was paid £17-13-6d 'for charges about the Lower House of Parliament'[2]. Some fifteen years later, Vowle wrote his account of the Elizabethan House of Commons, and in describing the Serjeant's various responsibilities said—*inter alia*—that 'he keepeth the door of the Inner House where the Commons sit, and seeth the same to be clean'.[3]

The absence of any positive information about the Serjeant's Housekeeping function before the end of Henry VIII's reign matches our ignorance of the other tasks performed by the Serjeants 'chosen by the Commons' during the same period. On the other hand, we know that valets (ushers) of the Parliament Chamber had been employed to prepare the Chamber and put up the necessary hangings and canopies for a meeting of Parliament; and there is a reference in the Issue Rolls of 1382 to two valets of the King's Household being rewarded 'for their labour and diligence continually staying at Westminster when the Parliament was held there, and waiting to guard the doors of the King's Chamber while the Parliament was there'.[4] John Bury, who was chosen by the Commons as their Serjeant sometime between 1461 and 1467, had previously been an usher of the Hall during the prolonged gap after Nicholas Maudit's death;[5] and it is possible that he would have been selected as Serjeant for both the 'housekeeping' and security experience he had acquired as an usher.

Until the 18th century the Serjeant had very little accommodation to administer on the Commons' behalf. Although King Edward VI had provided St. Stephen's Chapel as a chamber for the Commons, there were virtually no other rooms available for them for the next hundred years or so: Professor Neale has shown how there was only one committee room in the Palace at the disposal of Members and that as late as the reign of James I it was normal for the Committees to meet in suitable rooms or halls in the City or Inns of Court.[6] The House had in fact no space in which to expand in the mediaeval Palace: to the south lay the Lords, to the west the Law Courts in and around Westminster Hall, to the north the offices and residences of the Auditors and Tellers of the Exchequer, and to the east the Thames. At the beginning of the 18th century some small committee rooms were constructed above the cloisters, but it was clear that a more radical solution was necessary to the problem of finding adequate space for the two Houses.[7]

One such solution may have been suggested by Lovet Pearce's new Parliament House in Dublin, whose foundation stone was laid in 1728.[8] Its sensible layout showed what could be done with a purpose-built Legislature, and may well have persuaded Members at Westminster not to tinker with the mediaeval palace but to construct new Houses of Parliament to the east of Old Palace Yard, clearing away as much of the old buildings as was necessary and pushing back the river line to gain the requisite space.

William Kent was entrusted with the production of the plans and his first general scheme is dated 1732.[9] A number of alterations were made, and the second general scheme was approved by the Speaker in 1739. It would have provided a simple but dignified Palladian building for the Lords and Commons, and it would have included such innovations as division lobbies and a range of committee rooms along the river front, with interior courtyards used to provide proper lighting for each room, together with greatly improved galleries and toilet facilities.[10]

Nothing, however, on so large a scale was to be achieved: a series of wars, beginning with that with Spain in 1739, and Walpole's fall from power in 1743 meant that money was not available for the new building. Parliament had to wait until the fire of 1834 destroyed virtually all the old Palace before a completely new building could be erected.

Towards the end of the 18th century Soane did, however, manage to carry out a small part of Kent's plans, and this included the provision of a 'more commodious passage' into the House and a considerable number of committee rooms overlooking Old Palace Yard and St. Margaret Street.[11] The creation of these additional committee rooms brought their own problems: a Select Committee looking into the availability of committee rooms in 1832 found that four had been appropriated for purposes that had little to do with the Commons: one was occupied by the Poor Returns, another by the Court of Review, and two others by the Master of the Rolls and the Vice Chancellor of England—all very worthy persons or institutions, but their presence denied the use of those committee rooms to Members.[12]

12. Kent's plan for the new Houses of Parliament (1745)
(By kind permission of Sir John Soane's Museum)

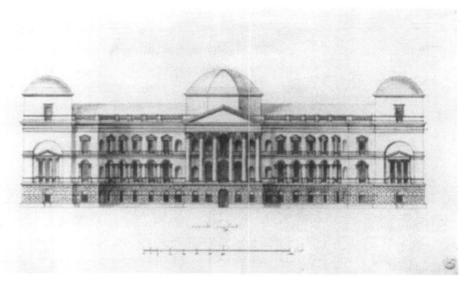

13. Barry's plan for enclosing New Palace Yard
(from a drawing in the House of Commons Library)

Whoever was at fault in allowing the encroachments, it was a clear demonstration of the need to uphold the principle that House of Commons facilities must be used for House of Commons purposes only.

Most people would have assumed that Sir Charles Barry's plans for the new Palace of Westminster after the 1834 fire would have provided everything that Members needed. But even before it was completed, Barry realised that the accommodation was going to be insufficient to meet the requirements of the two Houses and of Ministers. He therefore planned a gigantic office block to enclose New Palace Yard, and he was so determined to proceed with it that he left the lower floors of the Clock Tower faced in brick instead of stone, so that time and money would be saved if financial approval could be obtained. This was never given, and the Commons were left with increasingly inadequate accommodation.

In one respect, however, the Serjeant's Housekeeping burdens have been lightened since the Fire of 1834: before that he was responsible—through his Deputy Housekeeper—for providing refreshments for Members. The Bellamy family held this post at a modest profit for a number of years: they did not escape criticism but they attained everlasting fame with the dying Pitt's request for one of Bellamy's veal pies. After 1848, Members decided to run the catering themselves, initially through the Kitchen Committee, and latterly through the Select Committee on Catering.[13]

More recently, since the end of the 1939-1945 war, and as a result of pressure from Members, a number of schemes to provide substantially better accommodation have been produced by the Department of the Environment and its predecessors. In addition there have been many unofficial schemes thought up by outside bodies or by private individuals.

While most of the latter proposals have suggested resiting the House of Commons—or Parliament as a whole—in an entirely different location, the official schemes have concentrated on providing 'office blocks' for Members while leaving the layout of Barry's Palace more or less unchanged.

These latter have included plans for office blocks on the site of the present Abingdon Street Car Park; the corner of Bridge Street and the Embankment (Holford); the entire site between Whitehall and the Embankment (Spence & Webster); and the wide ranging Leslie Martin plan for redeveloping the whole of the area between the Ministry of Defence and Bridge Street—and the west side of Parliament Square—for Government offices, while providing some extra accommodation for the Commons on the north side of Bridge Street.

These schemes foundered, sometimes because they failed to win the full support of the House, but usually because the Government were unwilling to provide the necessary money.

The successive failure of the projects naturally caused considerable disappointment to Members; and the Department of the Environment, in conjunction with the authorities of the House, had to produce a number of *ad hoc* expedients to alleviate the growing pressure on space in the House. These included 'in-filling' schemes to provide extra rooms in the roof-space above the Committee Rooms or above the Members' Tea room in Commons Court, and in the Star Court range of offices alongside Westminster Hall. In addition a number of 'outbuildings' have been acquired to provide office accommodation for Members and Departments of the House, starting with 6 and 7 Old Palace Yard in 1959, and including a variety of other buildings such as the former Metropolitan Police Headquarters in New Scotland Yard—the Norman Shaw buildings—and the old Queen Anne's Bounty office in Deans Yard, and in 1992, No. 7 Millbank.

In 1984 the decision was made by the House of Commons Commission to refurbish the buildings on the east side of Parliament Street from Derby Gate southwards into Bridge Street to include St. Stephen's Tavern.

14. An interior of the Parliament Street Building (opened 1991).

15. The fine detailing of the entrance to 1 Derby Gate (New Parliamentary Building).

16. Michael Hopkins' design (centre) for the New Parliamentary Building, Phase II.

No. 1 Derby Gate, formerly the Welsh Office, became an extension of the Library; the two Georgian houses in the middle of the block were saved from the final stages of dilapidation to become residences for the Serjeant at Arms and his deputy, whose apartments in Speaker's Court were then vacated. The major part of the site on the corner of Parliament Square was modified to contain rooms for Members and secretaries, together with meeting rooms and substantial refreshment facilities. The Members' accommodation was named No. 1 Parliament Street and was opened by the Prince of Wales in November 1991.[15]

In 1992 the House approved the design of a completely new building to be sited at the junction of Victoria Embankment and Bridge Street. Before construction could begin it was necessary to put in place the infrastructure of the new and much expanded Westminster Underground Station which was to accommodate the Jubilee Line extension. The building was then built above the Station and in 1998 it was named Portcullis House; it will provide accommodation for some 200 members and their staff, together with Committee and meeting rooms and Library and Refreshment services. Portcullis House will be ready for occupation in late 2000.

NOTES TO CHAPTER FIVE

[1] *Commons Journals* 29, p. 631 (12 April 1763). Serjeant Odiarne's widow, Catherine, continued to hold the appointment of Housekeeper after Nicholas Bonfoy became Serjeant.

[2] *Acts of the Privy Councill* Vol. II p. 245.

[3] Vowle, quoted in Mountmorris *History of the Principal Transactions of the Irish Parliament* London 1792 pp. 123-124.

[4] *Issue Rolls* E 403/487 24th March 1382.

[5] *Rotuli Parliameniorum* Vol. V p. 159 1449.

[6] J. E. Neale. *Elizabethan House of Commons* London 1949 pp. 365–366.

[7] O. C Williams *Topography of the Old House of Commons* 1953. pp. 7 & 8.

[8] F. G. Hall *The Bank of Ireland 1783–1946* (Dublin 1949) p. 426.

[9] *Journal of the Royal Institute of British Architects* 6 August 1932. pp. 737–738.

[10] *Ibid* p. 746.

[11] O. C . Williams *op cit* p. 15.

[12] *Report of the Select Committee on the Library of the House of Commons Parl. Papers 1831–32 (HC 600), v, 318.*

[13] See Public Information Office *Factsheet* No. 53 for further details of the history of the Refreshment Department.

[14] See *Factsheet* No. 11 for further information on the Norman Shaw Buildings.

[15] See *Factsheet* No. 63 *The Parliament Street Building.*

Chapter six

Today's Duties

OUR UNFORTUNATE LACK OF KNOWLEDGE OF WHAT the Serjeants actually did for the Commons in the fifteenth century is equalled by the ignorance shown by most people about the role of a modern Serjeant at Arms. If questioned, the average person would say that he carries the mace in the Speaker's Procession, and performs other ceremonial duties. It is therefore the intention of this final chapter to explain what is involved in the maintenance of order and in housekeeping in the Precincts of the Commons, which are the principal tasks of the Serjeant described in the *Manual of Procedure*—see page viii. In discharging these responsibilities, the Serjeant is accountable both to the Speaker and to the House: as seen in Chapter II, he is appointed 'to attend upon the Speaker', but he is also described in Standing Orders as 'attending the House of Commons'.

In May 1990 the House of Commons Commission ordered an enquiry into the internal management of the House with a view to creating a co-ordinated management and decision-making structure to respond to Members' needs and demands for services and to determine priorities between them. Sir Robin Ibbs was invited to undertake this review. The major recommendations of the Ibbs Report published in November 1990 affecting the Department of the Serjeant at Arms were:

a. The establishment, under a Director of Finance, of systems of financial management, budgeting and control of expenditure. These systems are needed to monitor and influence spending procedures on all services for Members provided by departments of the House.

b. The formation of four domestic Select Committees, two of which: the Accommodation and Works Committee and the Administration Cormmittee, make policy recommendations to the House of Commons Commission on matters directly concerning the Department of the Serjeant at Arms. The Accommodation and Works Committee examines and approves the plans for major works in the House with regard to building maintenance, modification and updating of existing accommodation, as well as new projects such as the development on Bridge Street. The Administration Committee

17. Sir David Erskine on the Terrace, 1906 *(from a picture in the Palace of Westminster collection).*

deals with the provision of services to Members, regulations for access, filming and photography, car parking and so forth.

c. The establishment of a Director of Works, appointed to the Serjeant at Arms' Department. He is the professional adviser to the House on all works and accommodation matters; he prepares a programme of works for the Commission, through the Serjeant and the Accommodation and Works Committee. The Directorate of Works has assumed the responsibilities for the House previously undertaken by the Parliamentary Works Office and the Property Services Agency and fulfils an identical function for the House of Lords.

A further addition to the Department took place in 1996 when the Serjeant became responsible for the administration of the Directorate of Communications on behalf of both Houses. The Directorate has charge of the operation and development of the Parliamentary Data and Video Network, the telephone system, including voicemail and the Communications Help Desk, which serves all users of IT and telephone systems within the Palace and in constituencies, in the Scottish Parliament and the Welsh Assembly.

The Serjeants' office has been completely restructured and strengthened and there is now a Secretariat to back up the Serjeant, designed to achieve the required co-ordination of the Department's activities. It consists of an Executive Assistant (one of the Assistant Serjeants), a Finance Manager, an Information Systems Manager who also oversees the work of the Database Administrator, and a Fire Safety Manager. The Deputy Serjeant oversees the activities of what used to be the Serjeant at Arms Department (without the two Directorates) and at the time of writing we are trying to come up with a new title for what is really the third directorate of the enlarged Department.

In the maintenance of order, the Serjeant's main problem is the need to reconcile the conflicting requirements of security—ensuring the safety of the House (as well as the necessary degree of privacy for Members)—with those of access—imposing as few restrictions as possible on the requisite contacts between Members of Parliament and Strangers who, of course, include the Members' constituents.

To cope with the requirements of an ever-changing House, operating in a confined space, the Serjeant is involved, in consultation with the Administration Committee, in the amendment or formulation of regulations dealing with a wide variety of subjects, ranging from the important to the seemingly trivial, such as the carrying of photo-identity passes, the use of the underground car park, the categories of journalists who may be present in the Members' Lobby during the Sittings of the House, the hours of duty of the nurse, limitations on the use of House stationery, the booking of Committee Rooms, regulations for parties visiting the House, permits for video recorded interviews and photography, the hours of opening of the Transport Office and the availability of photocopying machines.

Although his Department is large and numbers some 400 (including about 180 in the Works Directorate) the Serjeant's responsibilities extend a long way beyond the work of those he directly employs. In maintaining order, for instance, the Doorkeepers of his Department are responsible for dealing with disturbances in the Galleries, while the Police and Security Officers, who act under his direction, are the employees of the Commissioner of Police for the Metropolis. Similarly, while many of his housekeeping tasks are discharged through his Office Keepers and Attendants, other tasks concerned with the maintenance of the building are performed by the staff of the Director of Works.

The arrangements for the admission of *Strangers* are complex. First and foremost are Press representatives and Members' staff, for whom accommodation is provided; then there are visitors who come by appointment to see Members individually or to attend meetings, or to obtain seats in the Galleries, or who are taken round the Palace by Members when neither House is sitting; there are Members' guests who have to be directed to the different dining or refreshment rooms; and there is the general public, who queue for seats in the Gallery or who may attempt to see a Member without prior notice. In addition, there are lobbyists who range from highly expert individuals and pressure groups to mass lobbyists who may come in very great numbers and who, except for the first thousand or so, cannot expect to achieve more than to stand in a slow moving queue outside the building.

The presence of a terrorist threat greatly complicates the task of assuring the fullest possible contacts between Members and the outside world. A number of additional precautions have to be taken: visitors have to be channelled through one entrance where security checks are enforced, and extra policing is necessary to ensure that people, once admitted into the Precincts, do not stray involuntarily or otherwise into the areas set apart for Members. The policing of the Palace, the six outbuildings and the areas surrounding the Precincts involves the fullest consultation between the Serjeant and the Metropolitan Police detachment in the Palace of Westminster, not only over the provision of Police and Security Officers for duty inside the Palace but also over the handling of Mass Lobbies.

The Serjeant's responsibilities for maintaining order do not extend beyond the Precincts, and the closest liaison with the outside Police is necessary to ensure that Mass Lobbies proceed in an orderly fashion and do not cause serious obstruction to Members entering or leaving the House. The advice of the police and security services is, of course, of the utmost importance in devising suitable anti-terrorist measures in the context of the Houses of Parliament.

In addition to maintaining order in the Galleries, the Serjeant has also to organise the issue of tickets to admit the Press and visitors. Applications for visitors are made by Members, and for the Press by the Editors of the newspapers and agencies concerned. There are separate Galleries for Peers and for Ambassadors and High Commissioners, who are admitted without tickets when they have identified themselves to the Police and the Doorkeepers. The Public have to queue in order to obtain seats in the Strangers' Gallery, if they have not previously obtained tickets from Members. The Serjeant's Office also maintains the Lobby List which gives the names of those who may be admitted to the Member's Lobby when the House is sitting. One section of this list deals with the press and broadcasting representatives who, as members of the Lobby, also attend ministerial meetings.

The Serjeant's main task as Housekeeper is to administer all the accommodation made available to the House of Commons in the Palace and in the various outbuildings except those rooms for which other departments like the Library and Refreshment Departments are responsible. The accommodation he looks after comes under five main headings: the Chamber, the 18 Committee Rooms and Interview and Conference Rooms; desks in Members' single, double or larger rooms in the Palace and outbuildings and also the spaces provided for Members' Private Secretaries and Research Assistants; the accommodation allotted to the Press Gallery; and the rooms containing facilities for Members such as the Television rooms, the Members' Cloakroom, the Hairdressing Salon and the changing and bathrooms.

This involves not only the servicing and cleaning of these rooms and their supervision and staffing by the Office Keepers and Attendants, but also their allocation. In the case of the Committee Rooms, the Serjeant's first priority is to see that rooms are made available for the various Standing and Select Committees of the House. Those not required for these purposes may be allotted to Members for private meetings in connection with parliamentary subjects.

Much inconvenience derives from the rule that Committees of the House have priority over private meetings, and from the fact that they often meet at short notice and can continue sitting even after the Rising of the House. Thus Members may find that the Committee Rooms they have booked—often many days in advance, and often for important meetings—have sometimes to be cancelled at less than 24 hours notice; and the Member must either abandon a meeting or transfer it to another time or day.

The shortage of accommodation near the Chamber affects the allocation of individual or shared rooms to Members. The Accommodation and Works Committee allots the available rooms among the various parties on the basis of their relative strength in the House; and the Party Whips, in consultation with the Serjeant's Office, have to decide to which Member a room should be allocated. Certain rooms, like those for Ministers, Whips and Party Leaders are allotted *ex-offcio* but the remainder are allocated on a basis of seniority and need, and much tact and patience are necessary to persuade Members that suitable rooms cannot be available for everyone until more office space becomes available.

In planning the occupancy of additional accommodation, whether it is in the form of existing buildings like the Norman Shaw blocks or an entirely new structure like Portcullis House, the Serjeant and his staff have to consult closely with the Whips and Members of Parliament appointed to the Accommodation and Works Committee to ensure that the new rooms and their furnishings and their access to the Chamber meet Members' requirements.

In an account of this comparatively short length, it is impossible to detail completely how the Serjeant carries out his day-to-day duties and what they are. Apart from attending the Speaker's daily meeting before the House sits, taking part in her procession into the Chamber with the Mace (the ceremonial) and regular duties in the Chair, he attends the meetings of four of the five domestic committees: Finance & Services, Accommodation & Works, Administration and Information. He is also a member of the Board of Management composed of the other five Heads of Department and liaises regularly with Black Rod, his opposite number in the House of Lords. The Serjeant deals with a huge variety of correspondence and personal queries from

Members, their staffs and the public; many members seek his advice and ask for his and his colleagues help with a wide spread of problems. He is the House's Executive Officer and Accommodation Officer and is responsible to, and under, the Speaker for good order and discipline throughout the House, regulating access by guests and the public who visit the Palace of Westminster, whether just to see Barry and Pugin's magnificent Gothic extravaganza, to meet their Member of Parliament, or to witness the democratic process in operation. All have a right to be properly looked after in safety, to work in an ordered, efficient and healthy environment and be provided with facilities worthy of a large legislative complex centred round a building designed in the 19th century coming rapidly to terms with the increasing demands of the technological age in which we now live.

In 1994 the first Conference of Commonwealth Serjeants at Arms was held in London and it is hoped that this will be a regular, five yearly occurrence. Regional Conferences are being scheduled too. The Canadian Serjeants meet annually in a different Province and the Australian Serjeant held a pan Pacific Conference of that area's Serjeants in 1996; more are planned. We see a regular stream of visitors, of fellow Serjeants, coming to London and a warm welcome awaits anyone who would like either to visit us for a few hours or a few days. The August 1999 Conference, again in London, takes place with some 35 visiting Serjeants, and in one or two instances their deputies, attending.

In today's world, all the evidence points to the fact that organisations which fail to adapt and change go to the wall; it is no good being in the grip of a time warp. It follows that one of the key tasks of the Serjeant at Arms is to ensure that the three elements of the Department move forward to ensure that everyone and everything is up with current best practice, and that the best value for money is being achieved. So, how would Maudit view the situation if he were alive today? One can only surmise, but he should be encouraged. Over the centuries the Serjeant's duties have evolved enormously. Although, like many of his overseas colleagues, security is one of the Serjeant's key responsibilities, he is still very much the Housekeeper. His present day duties can best be described as being 'administrative', very much at the centre of the House's affairs, co-ordinating the provision of many of the key services required by the House.

Yet the 'average person' mentioned at the beginning of this chapter is not wholly wrong: in spite of the Serjeant's administrative preoccupations, part of his time has to do with the various aspects of ceremonial. He, or one of his deputies, has to be present in the Chamber the whole time that the House, or a Committee of the whole House, is sitting. Primarily, he is there to execute the orders of the Speaker or the House, to supervise semi-routine drills like the conduct of Divisions and to deal with emergencies. But although his seat at the Bar also enables Members to bring him their queries and complaints, or ask him for tickets for vacant seats in the Galleries, the presence on the Floor of the Chamber of the Serjeant and the Mace serve as a constant reminder of the power available to the Speaker and the House if the need arises.

The Serjeant at Arms and his Department Extracts from Erskine May (22nd Edition)

THE APPOINTMENT OF THE SERJEANT AT ARMS IS IN the gift of the Queen, under a warrant from the Lord Chamberlain, and by patent under the Great Seal, 'to attend upon Her Majesty's person when there is no Parliament; and at the time of every Parliament, to attend upon the Speaker of the House of Commons'; but after his appointment he is the servant of the House and may be removed for misconduct. He ranks second in precedence among the permanent offices of the House. It is his duty to keep the gangway at and below the Bar clear, and to desire the Members to observe the rules of behaviour in the Chamber. He causes the removal of persons directed to withdraw; and gives orders to the door-keepers and others in connection with divisions. He also maintains order in the lobby and passages of the House and may be directed by the Speaker to ascertain and report on the facts when a disturbance has occurred. For the better execution of these duties he has a chair close to the Bar of the House. He also has the duty to give notice to all committees when the House proceeds to a division.

His ceremonial duties are to attend the Speaker, with the Mace, on entering and leaving the House, or going to the House of Lords, or attending Her Majesty with addresses; he introduces, with the Mace, peers or judges attending within the Bar, on presenting petitions; and brings up those called to the Bar to be examined, or to be reprimanded by the Speaker.

The Serjeant is also, by custom, Housekeeper of the House of Commons, a task which accounts for much of the work of his department. He has responsibility for the Parliamentary Works Directorate and the Communications Directorate.

The police on duty in the House are under his direction. He regulates, under the Speaker, the admission of persons to the Press Gallery and lobby and has control of the arrangements for the admission of strangers and for taking into custody those who gain access to the House irregularly, or misconduct themselves there.

Out of the House, he is entrusted with the execution of all warrants for the commitment of persons ordered into custody by the House, and for removing them to the Tower or a prison, or retaining them in his own custody. He serves, by his clerk in charge, as warrant officer of the House, all orders of the House, upon those whom they concern.

The Serjeant at Arms attends the Speaker and gives effect to the directions of the House. In addition to maintaining order and security in the Chamber, he is responsible for regulating security and access to the Commons area of the Palace of Westminster and the Parliamentary estate and for ensuring the provisions of the Sessional Order are met by the Commissioner of Police for the Metropolis. He is in charge of all accommodation and associated services for the Commons. In this, he is supported by a Senior Management Team comprising his Deputy, the Works Director, the Communications Director, the Head of Security and the three other Serjeants.

The Serjeant at Arms supervises the work of the Parliamentary Works and the Communications Directorates and is responsible for the Occupational Health Service. These provide services to both Houses. The *Parliamentary Works Directorate* is responsible for managing the programming and procurement of maintenance and new works and provides building, furnishings, cleaning, horticultural and curatorial services. The *Parliamentary Communications Directorate* is responsible for the strategic planning and implementation of electronic information services and provides common services for the Parliamentary networks which include data, video and telecommunications.

Organisation of Personnel in the Serjeant at Arms Department

Total: 395.5

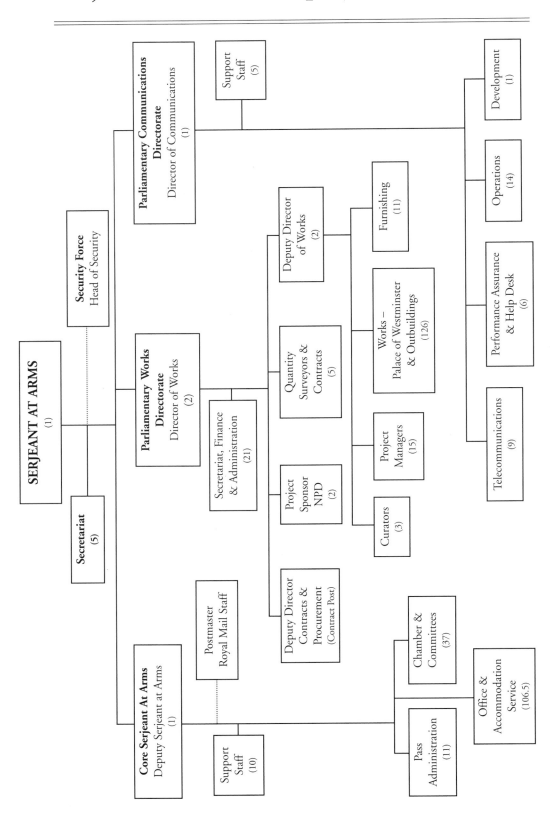

The development of Royal Maces

THE MACES OF NICHOLAS MAUDIT AND THE OTHER early Serjeants were both functional and symbolic; like the present day officers' swords, they were at the same time lethal and ceremonial—but gradually the warlike aspect of the Mace diminished, and increasing attention was paid to ornamentation. The Royal Arms became the most important part of the Mace; their design became more elaborate and, eventually, they were surrounded by a representation of the crown. The flanged head, having lost its warlike raison d'etre, decreased in size as well as usefulness, until it became smaller than the boss which bore the Royal Arms at the other end. When this stage was reached, it was no longer logical or convenient to hold the Mace with its head uppermost, and it became customary for the Serjeants to carry their Maces with the Royal Arms on top, and the erstwhile 'warhead' at the bottom.

It seems to have been the custom in the pre-Commonwealth days of the seventeenth century that each Serjeant-at-Arms in Ordinary of the Royal Household should provide his own Mace. Whenever a vacancy occurred in the Commons through the death or retirement of the Serjeant there, another of the Royal Serjeant-at-Arms was appointed to attend upon the Speaker, and he would bring his own Mace with him, and as fashions in the design of the Maces were continually changing each new Serjeant at Arms would bring a slightly different Mace to the Commons.

The 'Bauble' Mace that was made in 1649 represented a break with the past in a number of ways: it was ordered specially by the Commons because it had become necessary for the House to possess a Mace with the appropriate Commonwealth arms and ornamentation even though its general appearance was not so greatly different from the previous Royal Maces. In doing this the Commons also transferred the responsibility for providing the Mace from the Serjeants to the Exchequer, which henceforward was to pay for all the Maces used in the Commons. At the same time it was the first and only Mace whose design was approved by the Commons; hence the 'Bauble' designed by Maundy is the only Mace which can properly be called the 'House of Commons' Mace. None of the other Maces that have been used in the Commons, neither the pre-Commonwealth Maces provided by the Serjeants at Arms themselves nor those subsequently issued by the Jewel House, were expressly designed for the Commons.

The identification of the 'Bauble' Mace with the Commons may in fact have contributed to Cromwell's scorn for it. The Mace in the Commons had come, in seventeenth century eyes, to symbolise an element of authority which the Commons would not otherwise have possessed—deriving from the loan by the Head of State of a Serjeant at Arms with his power of arrest (c.f. Mr. Pym: 'Serjeant is an ensign of honour with which the King has been pleased to grace the Parliament.') Cromwell's memory of this may well have prompted him to make his celebrated remark, as the 1649 Mace did not come from the Head of State and consequently symbolised nothing more than the Long Parliament's sense of its own importance.

On the Restoration new Maces were ordered for the Royal Serjeants-at-Arms including the Serjeant attending the Speaker, but recent researches show that the Mace in the Commons was changed in 1670 and again in 1693. This need to replace and renew Royal Maces was due not only to any damage they may have suffered but also to the fact that as late as the time of George I it was still the custom for a Royal Mace to bear the arms and cypher of the reigning Sovereign; and this made it necessary to alter or re-make the Serjeants' Maces at the accession of a new Monarch. But at some period during the eighteenth century this practice was abandoned, and there are no Maces in the Regalia made after the death of George I. It is clear from the Jewel House records that the Maces used in the Commons have been changed at least six times since the end of the Commonwealth—the last time being in 1819 when the present Mace (originally made in 1660) was brought back. The fact that a Mace bearing the arms of Charles II was provided for the Commons at the end of the reign of George III does not appear to have evoked any comment.

Serjeants at Arms for the House of Commons 1415–1999

1415–1438	Nicholas Maudit	1717	Thomas Spence
1438–1461	Not known	1737	Wentworth Odiarne
1461	John Bury	1762	Nicholas Bonfoy
1471	Maurice Gethyn	1775	Edward Colman
1471	Robert Siddale	1805	Francis John Colman
1472	Nicolas Brytte	1812	Henry Seymour
1485	John Harper	1835	Sir William Gosset
1517	John Smythe	1845	Lord Charles Russell
1533	John St John	1875	Sir Ralph Gosset
1555	Thomas Hale	1885	Sir David Erskine
1576	Ralph Bowyer	1915	Sir Colin Keppel
1590	Roger Wood	1935	Sir Charles Howard
1610	Edward Grimstone	1957	Ivor Hughes[1]
1640	John Hunt	1962	Sir Alexander Gordon Lennox
1646	Edward Birkhead		
1660	Sir James Northfolk	1976	Sir Peter Thorne
1675	Sir William Bishop	1982	Sir Victor Le Fanu
1693	Samuel Powell	1989	Sir Alan Urwick
1709	Thomas Wybergh	1995	Peter Jennings

[1]Died before being knighted by the Queen

Printed in the United Kingdom for The Stationery Office